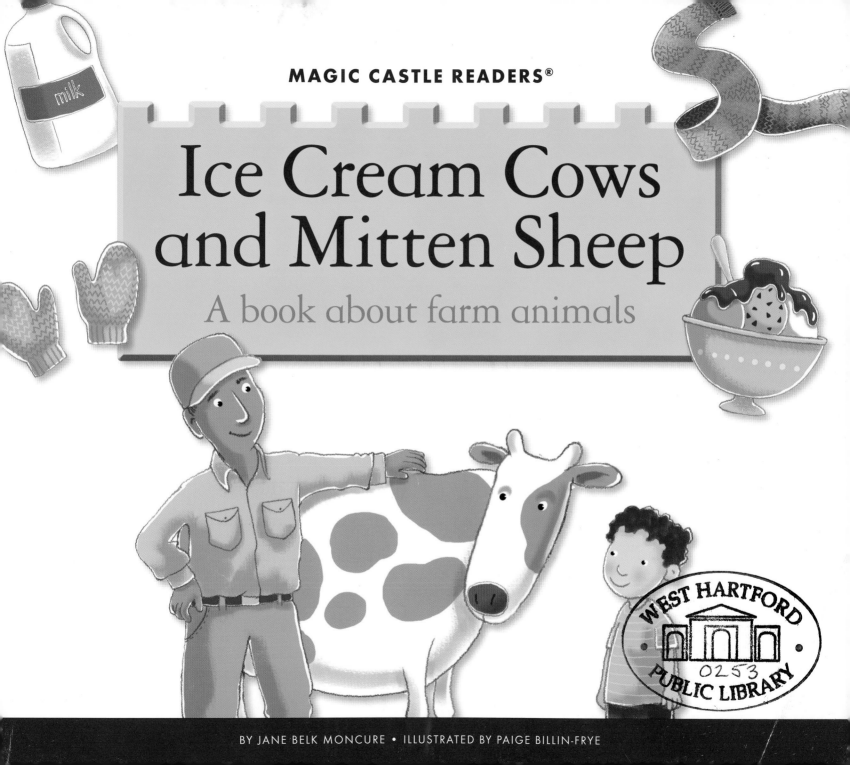

MAGIC CASTLE READERS®

Ice Cream Cows and Mitten Sheep

A book about farm animals

BY JANE BELK MONCURE • ILLUSTRATED BY PAIGE BILLIN-FRYE

The Child's World

Published by The Child's World®
1980 Lookout Drive • Mankato, MN 56003-1705
800-599-READ • www.childsworld.com

Acknowledgments
The Child's World®: Mary Berendes, Publishing Director
The Design Lab: Design
Jody Jensen Shaffer: Editing

ISBN 9781623235833
LCCN 2013931420

Printed in the United States of America
Mankato, MN
July 2013
PA02177

Did you know...

A library is a magic castle with many Word Windows in it?

What is a Word Window?

If you said, "A book," you're right!

A book is a Word Window because the words and pictures let you look and see many things. Books are your windows to the wide, wide world around you.

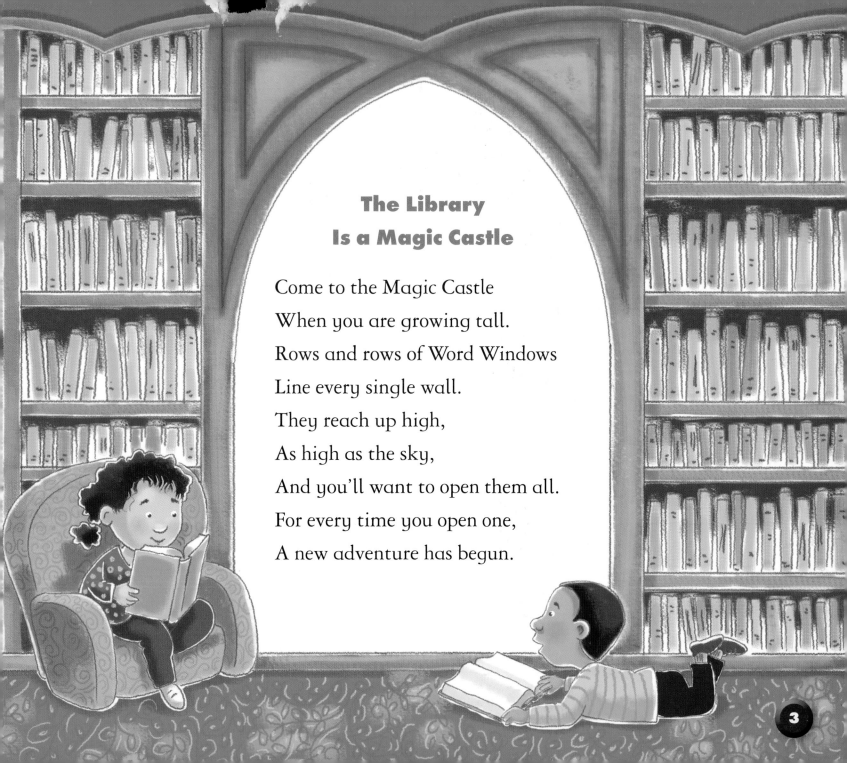

The Library
Is a Magic Castle

Come to the Magic Castle
When you are growing tall.
Rows and rows of Word Windows
Line every single wall.
They reach up high,
As high as the sky,
And you'll want to open them all.
For every time you open one,
A new adventure has begun.

David opened a Word Window.
Guess what David saw.

Cows. Lots of cows.
"Hi, cows," said David.

The cows were on their way to the barn.
So David went, too.

"Hi," said the farmer. "You are just in time
to see me milk the cows."

"What will you do with the milk?"
asked David.

"A milk truck will come. It will take the milk to the dairy," said the farmer.

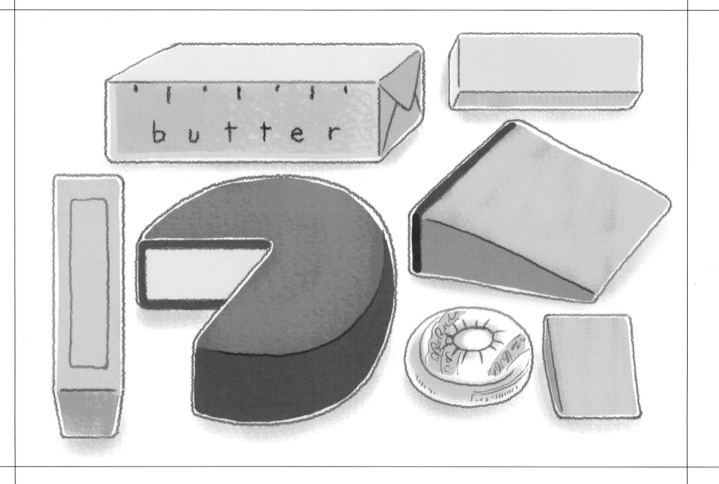

"At the dairy, the milk will be made into butter and cheese."

"It will also be made into milk to drink, yogurt, and ice cream for you," said the farmer.

David gave each cow a pat on the head.

"Thank you, cow," he said.
"Thanks for all you do for me."

Then David saw sheep, lots of sheep.
"Hi, sheep," he said.

The sheep were on their way to the barn.

David went, too.
"You are just in time to see me give haircuts
to my sheep," said the farmer.

BUZZ! BUZZ!
Off came the sheep's wool.

"What will you do with the wool?"
asked David.

"A truck will take the wool to the woolen mill,"
said the farmer.

"At the mill, the wool will be made into yarn.
All colors of yarn!"

"Yarn for a sweater, a scarf, a hat, socks,
and mittens for you," said the farmer.

David gave each sheep a pat on the head.

"Thank you, sheep," he said.
"Thanks for all you do for me."

Then David saw hens, lots of hens.
"Hi, hens," said David.

The hens were on their way to the henhouse.
David went, too. Guess what he found.

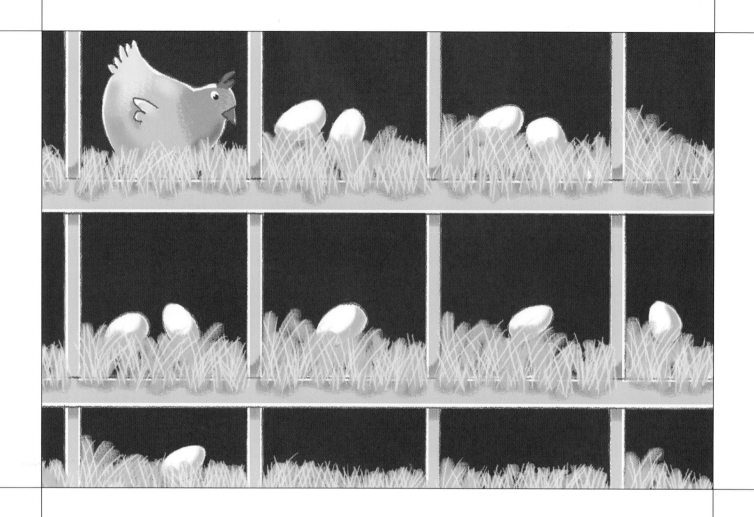

Eggs. Lots of eggs.

Eggs to fry, boil, scramble, and put in
an Easter basket.

What did David give each hen?
What did David say?

David wanted to stay at the farm,
but it was time to go home.

"Good-bye, farm friends!" said David.

Then David closed the Word Window.

Questions and Activities

(Write your answers on a sheet of paper.)

1. Where does this story happen?
    Name two important things about that place.

2. Name two things you learned about farm animals.
    What else would you like to know?

3. Did this story have any words you don't know?
    How can you find out what they mean?

4. Describe two characters in the story.
    Write two things about each one.

5. In one sentence, tell what this book is about.
    Name three ways the author tells the book's main idea.